Antarctica

Roger Kirkwood

Antarctica

Roger Kirkwood

A special thanks to all those expeditioners and others I have been to Antarctica with, who made my visits there so wonderful. Most important in getting me to Antarctica have been Tsutomo Ikeda, Harry Burton and Graham Robertson. I also thank the Australian Antarctic Division and Aurora Expeditions for taking me south.

In writing this book, I was assisted by the proofreading skills of Marjolein van Polanen Petel, Jodi Bagley and Richard Dakin. Also, I thank the friends who generously hunted out extra pictures for me: Dick Williams, John Kirkwood, Julie McMahon, Marjolein, Bec and Kieran Lawton, Doug Thost, Amanda Till, Tashi Tenzing, Beau Fahnle, Julie McInnes, Mark Curran, Frank O'Rourke, Chris Harrison, Graham Hosie, Greg Jenkins and Barb Clarkend. Jay Peter Kirkwood didn't help much, but kept me awake at night and smiled a lot.

I'd like to dedicate this book to my parents, Marj and Peter.

First published in Australia in 2008 by Young Reed
an imprint of New Holland Publishers (Australia) Pty Ltd
Sydney • Auckland • London • Cape Town

1/66 Gibbes St Chatswood NSW 2067 Australia
218 Lake Road Northcote Auckland 0627 New Zealand
86 Edgware Road London W2 2EA United Kingdom
80 McKenzie Street Cape Town 8001 South Africa

10 9 8 7 6 5 4 3 2 1

National Library of Australia Cataloguing-in-Publication Data:

Kirkwood, Roger.
        Antarctica.

        Bibliography.
        Includes index.
        For primary school students.
        ISBN 9781921073366 (hbk.).

        1. Antarctica. I. Title.

        919.89

Commissioning Editor: Yani Silvana
Designers: Hayley Norman and Tania Gomes
Production: Linda Bottari
Printer: Tien Wah Press, Malaysia

Picture Credits

t = top, b = bottom, c = centre, l = left, r = right
Doug Thost: pp. 9t, 13b.
Barb Clarkend: p. 12tr
Vin Morgan AAD: p. 12tl.
Harvey Marchant AAD: p. 14c (inset).
John Kirkwood: pp. 14cl; 24tl, tc, tr; 28b; 32b; 37cl
tussock; 42cl.
Greg Jenkins: p. 16cl.
Dick Williams: pp. 16c, b; 17cl, cr, b; 18c; 19t
Graham Robertson: p. 19b.
Frank O'Rourke: p. 29tl;
Kevin Bell AAD: p. 28cl.
Tashi Tenzing: p. 30 minke.
Beau Fahnle: p. 30 humpback; 31b.
Julie McInnes: p. 31cl.
Bec Lawton: p. 30r; 31c.
Marjolein van Polanen Petel: p. 21t; 37cr.
Chris Harrison: p. 40br.
Dan Eslake: p. 41br
Julie McMahon: p. 43r.

Douglas Mawson stamps reproduced with permission from
Australia Post: p. 9.

Contents

Antarctica
—a Rubber Duck?

Way down south on planet Earth there is a land that is very cold. It's called Antarctica. Antarctica is at the opposite end of the planet to the Arctic. Get it? Arctic—Ant-Arctic. The Arctic was named after a constellation of stars called Arktos (meaning 'the bear') which is in the sky above the Arctic. Coincidently, there are bears in the Arctic, Polar Bears. But, of course, there are no bears in Antarctica. Otherwise they would eat all the penguins.

Antarctica is shaped like a rubber duck. The peninsula is its bill. Can you see this on the map? A narrow neck separates West Antarctica (the head) from East Antarctica (the body). If all the ice were lifted off Antarctica, the east and west would be separated by a sea; it's just the ice that connects them.

Antarctic Circ

Cape Adare

Ross Sea

Mario Zuchelli (Italy)

Scott (NZ)

Magnetic South Pole in 1909

McMurdo (USA)

Dumont d'Urville (France)

Concordia (France/Italy)

Magnetic South Pole in 2005

Vostok (Russia

Lake Vostok

Casey (Aust.)

Australia

Zhongs (Chir

Mirny (Russia)

Davis (Aust.)

Southern Ocean

Maximum cover of **sea-ice** (Winter)

Minimum cover of sea-ice (Summer)

Ice-shelf

Antarctic stations

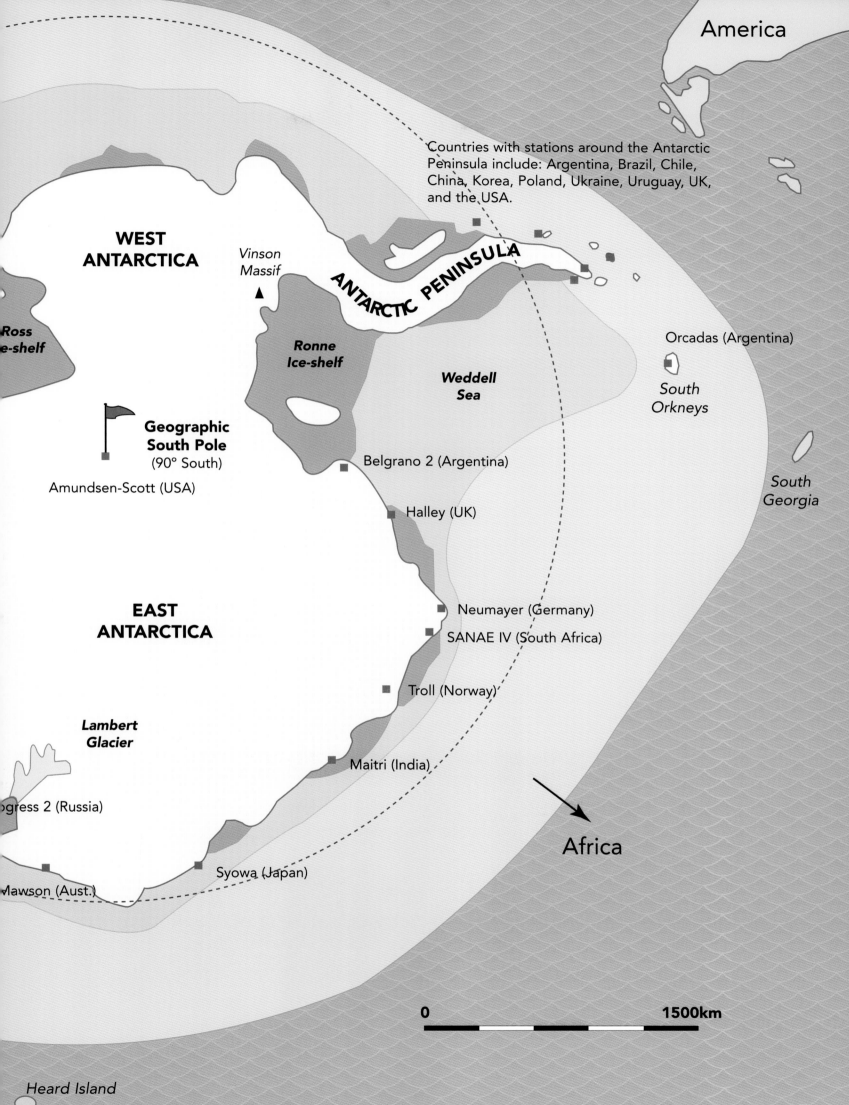

America

Countries with stations around the Antarctic Peninsula include: Argentina, Brazil, Chile, China, Korea, Poland, Ukraine, Uruguay, UK, and the USA.

WEST ANTARCTICA

Vinson Massif

ANTARCTIC PENINSULA

Ross Ice-shelf

Ronne Ice-shelf

Weddell Sea

Orcadas (Argentina)

South Orkneys

Geographic South Pole
(90° South)

Amundsen-Scott (USA)

Belgrano 2 (Argentina)

South Georgia

Halley (UK)

EAST ANTARCTICA

Neumayer (Germany)

SANAE IV (South Africa)

Troll (Norway)

Lambert Glacier

Maitri (India)

Africa

rogress 2 (Russia)

Syowa (Japan)

Mawson (Aust.)

0   1500km

Heard Island

Gondwana
Fragment Goes South

Did you know that about 200 million years ago Antarctica was warmer and covered in forests? It was part of a huge continent called Gondwana. A curious feature of continents is that they creep slowly around the Earth's surface. Sometimes they bump into one another and sometimes they tear apart. This movement is known as plate tectonics. Gradually, over millions of years, Gondwana broke up. Antarctica moved south towards the South Pole. By 40 million years ago, the other bits of Gondwana had crept north and Antarctica was isolated over the pole. It became cold and the forests disappeared.

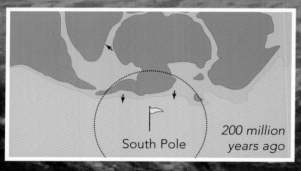

Gondwana 200 million years ago before it started to break up, showing the shapes of the continents it broke into. The arrows show the direction that the land was moving in. Can you tell which is Australia and which is Antarctica?

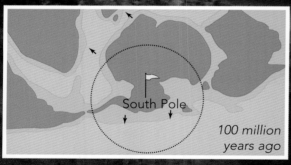

100 million years ago Africa and India broke away. Can you see how the land has changed its position relative to the South Pole?

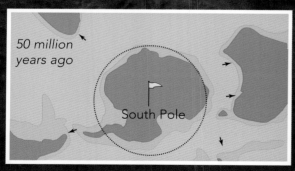

50 million years ago Antarctica settled into its currrent position. Australia and South America separated from it.

■ current land

■ **continental shelf**

■ sea

Heavy Seeds

There are clues that Antarctica was once joined to other continents. Lands that were part of Gondwana (Antarctica, Australia, South America, southern Africa and India) have rocks and fossils in common. One such fossil is *Glossopteris* (in Latin, *glosso* = tongue, *pteris* = fern), a fern-like plant that became extinct long ago. Seeds of *Glossopteris* were heavy, so they couldn't travel far by wind or water. So lands where you find *Glossopteris* fossils once were connected. Can you see the leaf pattern in the rock?

Forests of Antarctica

When Antarctica was part of Gondwana, it had forests of beech trees, cycads (fern-like trees) and conifers (pine trees—*Glossopteris* was actually a fern-like conifer). They would have looked similar to the forests that exist now in southern Chile. As the continent drifted south and got colder, fewer plants could survive. Antarctica's forests are now found only as fossils. The only living plants in Antarctica now are lichens, mosses and algae, and (would you believe it?) there are two sorts of flowering plants: a grass and a cushion plant (pictured).

Mountain Chains in the Sea

So what makes continents separate from each other? On the sea floor in the middle of most oceans there is a line of hills, called a mid-ocean ridge. They are in deep water, so you can't see the ridge tops. Each ridge line sits over a crack in the Earth's crust. Lava from inside the Earth spews into the crust around this crack. The lava cools to form new rock, pushing apart the crust at either side. The crust only moves apart at less than 1 centimetre each year. But over millions of years this adds up to a lot of moving.

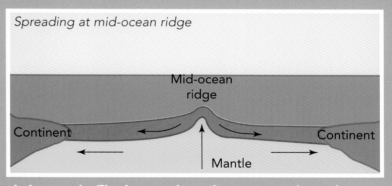

Spreading at mid-ocean ridge

Mid-ocean ridge

Continent

Continent

Mantle

Colliding Crusts

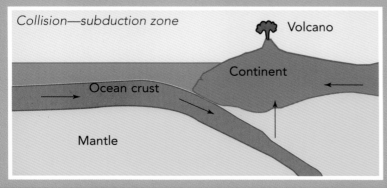

Collision—subduction zone

Volcano

Continent

Ocean crust

Mantle

While some new crust is being formed in mid-ocean ridges, other crust is being lost elsewhere. Where two continents collide, big mountains form. Can you think of a place where this could be happening? Where a piece of continental crust collides with ocean crust, the continent floats on top and the ocean crust is pushed down. This is called a **subduction zone.** If ocean crust meets ocean crust, one will slide over the top of the other.

Cold Continent

Not much snow falls on Antarctica each year, but the snow that does fall stays there a long time. Millions of years worth of snow has formed the **Antarctic ice-sheet**. In some places this sheet is over 4 kilometres thick. Snow has filled the valleys, smothered the plains and covered the hills of what was once a continent of forests. Only the tops of mountains poke through now.

Emperor Penguins *huddle together against a freezing Antarctic blizzard.*

Antarctic Winds

Warm air rises, cold air sinks, and over Antarctica there is a lot of cold air. This blows down the **Antarctic ice-sheet** towards the coast, reaching speeds of over 300 kilometres an hour. That's three times the speed your car goes. When the wind is very fast and filled with so much snow that you can't see anything, it's called a **blizzard**.

Is Antarctica Really the Driest Place?

Driest! How can you call Antarctica the driest when the ice there represents 70 per cent of the Earth's fresh water? It's said to be driest because it hardly ever rains in Antarctica. In fact, rain falls just 20 days a year on the peninsula and never over East Antarctica. Snow and ice falls, but just 150 millimetres each year. How does this compare with the rainfall where you live?

A rare rainy day in Antarctica.

This seal has died and dried out in the dry Antarctic atmosphere.

A World Below the Ice

Underneath several kilometres of ice on the Antarctic Plateau near Russia's Vostok Station, there is a huge lake called Lake Vostok. Warmed by the land underneath and kept liquid by the pressure of ice on top, Lake Vostok is mysterious. Researchers could drill down to it but they have to be careful. They don't want to contaminate the lake. Whatever is there has not been disturbed for millions of years. It could give clues to life on other planets with similar conditions: high pressure, no oxygen, no light, calm... What lives there? Anything? What do you think an animal living there might look like?

Is Antarctica Really the Highest Place?

Why do people say this? The highest peak in Antarctica is Vinson Massif, which is about 5000 metres tall. Although high, Vinson would be just a hill in the Himalayas, where mountains are more than 8000 metres high. Antarctica is called the highest continent because the enormous **ice-sheet** covering it gives it an average height of 2300 metres. That's 1000 metres (1 kilometre) higher than the average height of any other continent. It's even higher than Australia's highest point (Mt Kosciuszko, at 2228 metres).

Antarctica Is Cold!

In Antarctica, the sun is low in the sky during summer and below the horizon for much of winter. With so little sun, it's very cold. Temperatures rarely get above 0°C. Along the coast, the temperature averages −10°C but inland it gets much colder. The lowest temperature recorded on Earth was −89.6°C at Russia's Vostok Station in inland Antarctica. Compare that with your average fridge (4°C) and freezer (−15°C).

Bubbles Trapped in Ice

Antarctic ice is formed from snow and there are air gaps in snow crystals. The snow is squashed flat when more snow falls on top of it. During squashing, snow crystals turn to ice and the air collects into bubbles. The deeper you go down into Antarctic ice, the older the bubbles. Researchers have drilled down and pulled out long columns of ice, called ice-cores. Scientists can test air in the bubbles to see what the air on Earth was like thousands of years ago and how it has changed over time. In the last 100 years, there has been an enormous rise in the level of carbon in the Earth's air. This rise could be caused by humans. Humans might make more carbon in the air by burning lots of coal, oil, gas and petrol.

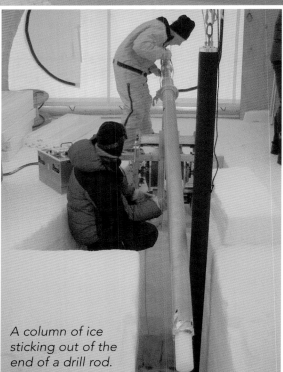

A column of ice sticking out of the end of a drill rod.

Rocks Trapped in Ice

Glaciers scrape over the surface of Antarctica, grinding away the land. They collect a lot of dirt and rocks. As **glaciers** pass mountains, rocks are collected from them too. Like rivers of water, rivers of ice transport lots of dirt and rocks to the sea.

A glacier enters the sea.

Icebergs

The ends of **glacier tongues** and **ice-shelves** break off and float free as **icebergs**. Initially, icebergs stay upright with flat tops and are called tabular (table-like). Soon they start to melt, break up and roll over. A lot of the melting happens underwater. Around Antarctica there are thousands of giant icebergs. An iceberg floats higher than your average ice-cube in a glass of water; almost one-eighth of it sits out of the water. This is because of the trapped air bubbles, and because icebergs are made of fresh water, so they float in the **denser** sea water.

Rivers of Ice

Ice on Antarctica is moving slowly towards the edges. In Antarctica's valleys, it forms rivers of ice, or glaciers. The biggest glacier in the world is the 400-kilometre long and 65-kilometre wide Lambert Glacier. Different glaciers move at different speeds. Some can flow slowly and smoothly 1–2 metres each year. Others can be frantic, grumbling and groaning downhill at speeds of more than 60 metres a year.

Watch Out for Crevasses!

As glaciers move, they twist, bend and buckle. Gaps called crevasses open up and close again. You might step over some crevasses without thinking about it; others could swallow a horse and some could swallow a jumbo jet. Sometimes, wind-blown snow accumulates over crevasses and hides them. Crevasses can be deep, even over 100 metres. That's a long way to fall. So if you walk over Antarctica, you have to watch out for crevasses.

An expeditioner looks over heavily crevassed ice, planning the safest route across.

Icy Tongues

Closer to the coast, the air is warmer. The surface of the ice evaporates a bit and on warm days a lot of ice can melt. Freshwater rivers can tumble down into crevasses and eventually run into the sea. When a glacier reaches the coast, it can float out onto the ocean. It looks like a big, icy tongue. It's called a **glacier tongue**. In places where glacier tongues are close together, they can join up to form enormous **ice-shelves** over the sea. Ice-shelves can be more than 100 metres thick. Look at the map of Antarctica; can you see where there are some ice-shelves?

Measuring Water Currents

Scientists can track water currents in the Southern Ocean in several ways. For example, satellites can measure sea-surface temperature. Floating buoys that drift in currents can take readings from their environment and send information to satellites. Another tool is the Conductivity—Temperature—Depth measurer or CTD. Conductivity provides a measure of saltiness. A CTD in the sea can record how salty and cold the water gets.

A CTD is lifted from the sea after taking measurements.

Green Soup

Did you know that most of the **photosynthesis** on Earth happens in the ocean? Thousands of **microscopic** plants called **phytoplankton** live in every bucket of sea water. These plants need sunshine to grow. Can you imagine what happens to them in the Southern Ocean in winter? When there is a cover of sea-ice blocking out what little sunshine there is, the phytoplankton don't like it—many die off. Without phytoplankton the sea becomes amazingly clear. In summer the opposite happens. With lots of sun and no sea-ice the phytoplankton can multiply very quickly. The sea turns into a green phytoplankton soup.

This is what the phytoplankton look like under a microscope.

There's very little sun in the Antarctic in winter.

Walking on Water

Sea-ice has amazing strength. When it is just a few centimetres thick, it will support your weight. When it's 5 centimetres thick, you can jump up and down on it and make ripples that spread out across the surface. But if you jump too much the ice will crack and you will fall through! When sea-ice is 30 centimetres thick, you can safely drive over it on a four-wheel motorbike. Would you feel safe out over the sea walking on thin sea-ice or driving a motorbike on it?

The Ocean's Skin Freezes

Each winter, the surface of the ocean around Antarctica freezes. Sea water freezes at –1.8°C. Freezing starts on still, cold days in Autumn. First, small ice crystals form. These grow into a slurry. The crystals join together to form a thin skin, called sea-ice. Gradually, more sea water freezes to its base and it thickens. By November, the ice skin over the ocean is about 2 metres thick. In places, though, the sea-ice is pushed together by wind and currents. It buckles into ridges that can be more than 10 metres thick. Not many ships can bust through that sort of sea-ice; some that try get stuck. In November, the sun warms and weakens the sea-ice. Waves and tides break it up and winds blow it away from the coast. It melts away out at sea.

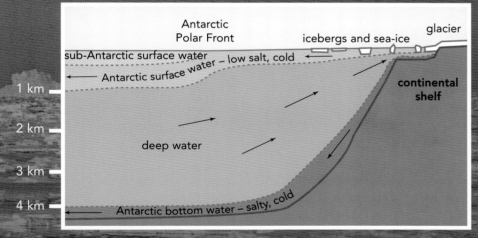

Cold Bottom Water

Salt water is heavier than fresh water. As seawater turns to ice, salt is forced out. The cold water below the ice gets saltier and, therefore, heavier. So it sinks. Formation of sea-ice around Antarctica causes billions of litres of cold, super-salty water to sink to the bottom of the ocean. Seawater freezing to the base of **glacier tongues** and **ice-shelves** does the same thing. This cold, super-salty water forms a current of 'Antarctic bottom water' that travels north and crosses the equator. It eventually comes to the surface in the Northern Hemisphere.

Cold Surface Water

In summer, sea-ice and **icebergs** melt. On land, melting snow and ice create rivers of fresh water. These flow out from underneath glacier tongues and form a surface layer of less salty sea water on the ocean. Like the bottom water (see above), this becomes a current that moves north. In the middle of the Southern Ocean, this cold surface current meets warmer northern waters. This region is called the **Antarctic Polar Front**. The colder Antarctic water sinks below the warmer water and continues to travel north. Eventually it resurfaces around continents like Australia, Africa and South America. Meanwhile, the main current of the Southern Ocean is spiralling around Antarctica from west to east. It takes 7–11 years to drift a full lap.

On a sunny summer day lots of ice melts.

Creepy Little Critters

Oceans are filled with amazing little animals called zooplankton that you hardly ever hear about. You need a microscope to see many of them. Some are long and thin, others are round and jelly-like and some look like tiny army tanks. They drift with the currents and eat phytoplankton, or each other. Many Antarctic zooplankton are giants compared to similar critters elsewhere. Their larger size helps them survive between feeds during long, dark winters when food is hard to find.

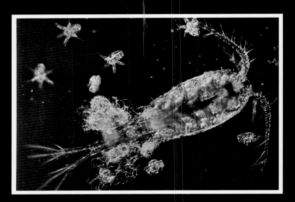

Antenna Heads

The most abundant animals in the world would have to be **copepods**. Trillions of these tiny **crustaceans** (crab-like creatures) live in all the world's oceans. They feed on phytoplankton and are eaten by bigger zooplankton, fish and seabirds. Sticking out the top of their heads, copepods have two long antennae that they use for swimming. The antennae twitch and look sort of like they're doing breast-stroke. And copepods have a single eye-spot in the middle of their head. Baby copepods look like balls with little arms.

Armour-plated Zooplankton

Built like tiny army tanks, **amphipods** patrol the seas looking for things to eat. Some are **parasites** on fish. We know amphipods best as sea lice that live under seaweed on the beach or zoom across rock pools. In Antarctica there is a giant amphipod (pictured) that is as big as your fist. This beast has huge eyes and lurks and hunts deep in the dark waters.

Jelly Blobs with Stomachs

Salps are jelly blobs that can be pea-sized or football-sized. They have a round stomach, often orange or green in colour. Around the stomach they build a clear jelly filter basket with a hard outer surface. The basket has a hole at either end that lets sea water move through. Salps filter phytoplankton and small zooplankton out of the water using strands of jelly that pass into their stomach. There are heaps of salps. They survive in **nutrient**-poor waters where not many other zooplankton can live. Salps reproduce by building a long chain of 'mini-me's'. When the mini-me's get big enough, they separate from one another.

Krill Fishery

Even though krill are small, people fish for them. The Soviet Union used to catch the most krill; they used them as ground fertiliser and pig food. When the government stopped giving fishermen cheap fuel for their boats, the fishermen couldn't afford to go to Antarctica anymore just for pig food, so they stopped going. But krill are still fished for human food; they are eaten mainly in Japan. Krill are tricky to prepare for eating. Soon after capture, they turn mushy, and fluorine (a toxic chemical) gets into their flesh. Also, their hard body covering (or **exoskeleton**) is hard to peel off.

A krill net comes on board a research vessel.

Super Krill

Krill are shrimp-like creatures that whales love to eat. Lucky for the whales down south, there are tonnes of krill in the Southern Ocean. In fact the biggest krill in the world live there, **Superb Krill**. These grow to 6 centimetres long. During summer, Superb Krill form huge schools, sometimes more than a kilometre wide. Each krill kicks along using five pairs of legs, called pleopods. At the same time, they filter phytoplankton out of the sea using a basket arrangement of their six pairs of hairy arms. Fancy having five pairs of legs and six pairs of hairy arms! Krill are at the centre of the Antarctic food chain. As well as being whale food, Antarctic fish, birds and seals eat them too.

Bristly Worms

There is a worm that swims in the ocean. It is small, has many legs and many bristles and is called a **bristle worm**. Swimming bristle worms like to eat **copepods**.

Toothy Mouths

There's a group of strange arrow-shaped animals in the ocean called **chaetognaths** (prounounced *key-tog-naths*). Some Antarctic chaetognaths grow to 15 centimetres long. They are ferocious carnivores (meat-eaters). The mouth at the top of their head is surrounded with savage, grasping spines. Any small krill or copepod that gets close to them needs to watch out! Can you see the krill

Fishy Stories

As Antarctica drifted south and the seas around it got colder (see page 8), not many fish hung around. The cold water and the great expanse of the Southern Ocean stopped other fish coming in from warmer waters. With few other sorts of fish in Antarctica, one group did particularly well: the notothenids (pronounced no-toe-theen-ids).

What Is a Notothenid?

Notothenids are bony, perch-like fish that live only in Antarctica. Most of the 200 species of fish in Antarctica are Notothenids. Some are big and some are small. Some live near the surface but most live near the bottom. They all have big mouths. After all, if something tasty comes along, you want to be able to fit it in your mouth—it might be a long time until the next meal. Notothenids make a substance called glycoprotein in their blood that stops their blood freezing. Just like anti-freeze in your car! This lets notothenids survive in water colder than 0°C.

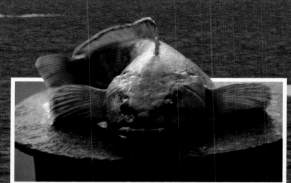

Going to School with Antarctic Herring

Antarctic Herring form large schools around Antarctica. This notothenid is the most common fish in the mid-water of the **continental shelf**. Emperor Penguins find them delicious.

Giant Kondakovia

In the depths of the Southern Ocean is a giant squid that hasn't got a simple name: it's called **Kondakovia longimana**. Imagine a squid the size of a man, with tentacles up to 8 metres long! We don't know much about *Kondakovia* because they are hard to catch. They eat slow fish and are eaten by toothed whales and Elephant Seals. When these squid die, they float. Surface **scavengers**, like many of the Antarctic birds, love to feast on dead *Kondakovia* floating on the surface.

Fish that Glow in the Dark

Lanternfish don't really have lanterns. Instead, they have lots of **fluorescent** spots over their bodies. The spots help them find each other; they can also confuse a predator trying to eat them. Lanternfish are small but super-abundant just off the **continental shelf** and near the **Antarctic Polar Front**. During the night, they swim up towards the surface to feed. During the day, they dive deep to avoid predators. Elephant Seals and King Penguins like to eat lanternfish.

Annual Squid

Squid are hungry hunters of fish and smaller squid. They grow fast— many breed when only one year old and then die of old age. In the Southern Ocean there are big squid fisheries. Close to Antarctica though, the squid are either too hard to catch or too small, so not many fishermen go after them. The most abundant squid around the edge of the continental shelf is Glacier Squid. It feeds on krill and Antarctic Herring and is eaten by penguins.

Living in Ice-castles

One secretive notothenid is the **Bald Notothen**. Bald Notothens live under the ice and love it when the ice starts to melt. They patrol the many tunnels and caverns that form as the ice melts, in search of crunchy **crustaceans**, like **amphipods** and **copepods**. But they have to watch out for Weddell Seals: some smart Weddell Seals learn to blow bubbles into the tunnels and scare Notothens out. Then the seal eats them. Can you see the head of the fish sticking out of the net?

Toothfish

Toothfish are the biggest fish in Antarctica. Males grow to 1.5 metres. Females can be more than 2 metres long. Toothfish live for more than 50 years. They eat mostly smaller fish and make delicious meals for Weddell Seals. Toothfish are also easily caught by fishermen. Being long-lived and easily caught means they could quickly be over-fished. Pretty soon there might not be many toothfish left.

Flappers and Gliders

Travelling over the big oceans to Antarctica, you might think you won't see much life. But you'd be wrong. Rarely does an hour go by without seeing a bird and often there will be hundreds. Little ones and heavy ones have to flap a lot, but many medium-sized and bigger birds also glide. Gliders can cover thousands of kilometres using little energy. Can you pick which of these birds are flappers and which are gliders?

Flying Chessboards

The **Cape Petrel** is a magnificent high-speed flier, skimming the water, zooming past ships and banking and turning like a jet fighter. Distinctive and common right across the Southern Ocean, these black and white birds resemble flying chessboards. Although appearing small against the waves, a Cape Petrel's wing span is 60 centimetres. Cape Petrels nest on cliffs along the Antarctic coast and on many islands.

Butterflies of the Open Ocean

Dancing and flitting across the waves are black and white butterflies of the sea, the **Wilson's Storm Petrels**. When you see how small they are (weight 35 grams, wing-span 35 centimetre) and how much energy they seem to burn up, it's hard to imagine they survive. Storm Petrels feed on tiny things floating in the top centimetre of the ocean—**copepods**, chaetognaths, fragments of meat from dead things. Little bits of floating plastic that look like food are a nightmare for the petrel's digestion.

Chooks of the Antarctic

Probably the most bizarre bird you will find in Antarctica is the cheeky little **Sheathbill**. It resembles something between a pigeon and a chicken. Sheathbills are the only birds in Antarctica that do not have webbed feet. They will eat pretty well anything, including some smelly stuff, like poo and long-dead animals. Despite eating such muck, and scurrying around in muddy penguin colonies, Sheathbills keep themselves crispy clean and white.

Seabirds with Attitude

Skuas are strong fast fliers, and feared feisty hunters. They will eat burrowing petrels, Snow Petrels and penguin chicks. They also eat **zooplankton**, fish and even pieces of dead animals. Skuas get grumpy if you get too close to their nests and will dive-bomb you, like magpies and lapwings sometimes do.

Angels of the Ice

Snow Petrels are beautiful, pure white birds with black eyes and a black bill. Being white, Snow Petrels can be hard to see against **sea-ice** and **icebergs**. They nest in cracks in rocks, often near the coast. Some also fly hundreds of kilometres inland to nest at isolated mountain peaks. Snow Petrels have even been seen at the Geographic South Pole.

Burrowing Petrels

Antarctic Petrel

Each night during summer at most **sub-Antarctic** islands, the skies fill with burrowing petrels returning to their nests. They dig long burrows to nest underground and hide from birds like Skuas that want to eat them. Once they have a good burrow they will return to it year after year to lay eggs and raise chicks. Burrowing petrels include Antarctic Petrels, Prions, Diving Petrels and Blue Petrels. You can only tell some species apart by the different colour patterns on their faces. But you can be sure they can tell each other apart.

The Coldest Cormorants

Imperial Cormorants are so heavy that they have to flap like crazy to stay above the waves. They are heavy because they have lots of swimming muscles, which makes them and other cormorants great divers. With their wings folded up and kicking out with their large webbed feet, they chase fish and krill down to depths of 60 metres. Imperial Cormorants make nests of seaweed on coastal cliffs of the Antarctic Peninsula and **sub-Antarctic** islands.

Big Gliders

Some big Antarctic birds need wind to help them fly. In calm weather they have to sit on the water and wait. When the wind blows, they stretch out their wings and get lifted up into the air. With just a few flaps they are off. Then they glide. They can glide huge distances—up to 1000 kilometres in a day. These big gliders mostly have their nests, where their chicks are raised, on sub-Antarctic islands.

Wandering around the World

'Holy mackerel, that's a big bird', you'd think if you saw a **Wandering Albatross**. With a wingspan of 3.5 metres, these are the largest flying birds in Antarctica. Measure that out in your lounge-room. It's big! Wanderers glide effortlessly above the waves, riding the winds for hundreds of kilometres each day. The Southern Ocean is a big backyard for them. Wanderers take about 15 months to raise a single chick, so they breed only every second year. They try to keep the same partner for life.

Exquisite Grey-headed

Grey-headed Albatrosses have a wing span of 2.5 metres, as do most albatrosses. Their heads are a smokey-grey and their bills are black and yellow-striped. They are just beautiful. They breed and raise a chick every two years. During their off-year, they may completely circle Antarctica.

Superb Light-mantled Sooty

Albatrosses generally nest in colonies, but not the **Light-mantled Sooty Albatross**. These magnificent birds nest on isolated cliff ledges. To attract a partner to its nest, the male produces an eerie wail, with a little intake of breath at the end—ooooaaahhhh……hee!! If the female is attracted, the pair bond and perform a spectacular display of flying around close together without crashing.

Long-lines the End of the Line

Long-line fishing is horrible for many Antarctic birds. A line can be more than 20 kilometres long with thousands of baited hooks attached. As the lines go out, seabirds eat the bait and get dragged underwater and drown. Tens of thousands of albatrosses, giant petrels and other seabirds drown every year on long-lines. This is one of the biggest environmental concerns in Antarctic waters.

Giant Petrels

Giant Petrels are big birds, bigger than some albatrosses. Their wing span is about 2.5 metres and they weigh nearly 5 kilograms. Giant petrels have large, powerful beaks. With these, they can quickly eat bodies of dead seals, kill and eat small penguins, and compete well with other birds for food on the surface of the ocean. Young Giant Petrels are a chocolate brown colour. As the birds mature the feathers around their head and neck become a light grey colour—a bit like humans.

Some Giant Petrels are all white.

Black-browed Albatross *chicks*

Patient Chicks

Mum and Dad have flown away over the horizon. They could be feeding a thousand kilometres away. So what do you think you'll get up to? Well, not much if you're an albatross chick. Just sit and wait and trust that the folks will return. And they do, maybe once a week. If a Skua comes by looking to eat you, you could throw-up a warm, sticky vomit on it. The messy looking Skua will spend hours trying to clean the vomit off.

Majestic Black-broweds

From a distance, you can't tell **Black-browed Albatrosses** apart, but close up, they all have slightly different black eyebrows. Their wonderful beaks are coloured pastel pink and orange. In young birds, though, the beak is a smoky colour. Black-broweds build a fancy bowl-shaped nest out of mud and vegetation. They may use the nest year after year. Parents bring back food and regurgitate it for the chicks. The chicks grow quickly.

Meet the Brushtails
There are three types of brushtail penguins.

Gentoo

Chinstrap

Adelie

Catch a Partner

Male penguins arrive at the suburbs first. Clever male penguins try to find the best place for a nest. Somewhere with lots of stones, perhaps near the centre of the suburb rather than the edge, safer from Skua attacks. Males try to beat any newcomers to the site where they nested last year. Near to last year's nest, they will build a pile of stones and try to attract any passing female. Once partnered the female tests out the nest of stones and soon after lays two eggs. Chicks hatch after 30–35 days and **fledge** 60 days later. From then on they look after themselves.

A male **Adelie Penguin** (left) tries to impress a female with the nest he has built.

Adelie Penguin

Stone Exchange

Stones are important in penguin suburbs. They keep the eggs and chicks out of melt water that could gather at the suburb. Penguins that arrive late try to pinch stones from the early arrivers. Lots of stone stealing can lead to fights between neighbours.

Adelie Penguin

24

Suburban Lives

Each spring around the coast of Antarctica, hoards of penguins gather to breed in huge penguin 'suburbs'. The sites they choose are near to where there is lots of food. They also like to hang out where snow melts early to expose the ground and hopefully lots of stones (stones are important for nest-building). The penguins that gather are collectively called brushtails because they have long tail feathers that sweep from side to side as they walk.

Chick Down

Penguin chicks, such as these **Adelies**, have a thick, warm coat of fluffy feathers called down. This coat is perfect for roaming around the suburbs, but it can get grubby. When it is nearly time to go to sea, the chicks **moult** off the down. Underneath is a crispy new coat of strong feathers, just like their parents'. Moulting must be uncomfortable. Penguins scratch a lot and get cranky when they are moulting.

Adelie Penguins

Chicky Chase

When the chicks get big enough they can leave the nest. If a parent arrives home, the chicks will chase it all over the colony. The chicks fall over all the time and the parent looks stressed. It runs away to make sure the chicks grow strong and fast. A very funny sight!

25

Huddling

Huddling together is crucial to the survival of Emperor Penguins. While in a huddle, a penguin is warmer and uses half the energy of penguins standing outside the huddle. Males huddle to survive the long winter without feeding. Chicks huddle to survive cold nights when their parents leave them at the colony. Huddles can get so tight that penguins in the middle get squished. They raise their beaks and call 'Hey, stop shoving!', or the penguin equivalent. But once they move to the outside, it's not too long before they are cold and try to get back in.

Race of the Male Emperor Penguin

Try this! Hold a ball of socks between your ankles—that's your egg. Now try to walk around. That's about as fast as a male Emperor Penguin can go. Pretend it is −30°C. You don't want to lose the egg for even a minute or it will freeze. Don't panic now, but it looks like that big **iceberg** beside you might role over on top of you. You have to move away fast! Shuffle...shuffle...shuffle. Now huddle together for warmth, but DON'T LOSE THAT EGG.

Immaculate Girls

Through the darkness of winter, across the **sea-ice**, quietly, reliably...a big, pristine, female **Emperor Penguin** returns to her colony. It's a 100 kilometre walk. For the past two months, she has chased food in the sea during the four hours of light of each winter's day and rested on the ice during the 20-hour-long nights. On arrival at the colony, in front of thousands of expectant males, she gracefully bows her head and trumpets, calling to her partner.

Emperors of Winter

Emperor Penguins are inspirational. They are the only animals to breed during the Antarctic winter. They go through a lot of hardship to raise their chicks.

Breeding Cycle

Emperor Penguins gather at colonies on the **sea-ice** in April. After a period of getting to know a partner, the female lays a single 250 gram egg. She gives it to the male and leaves for two months. The male balances the egg on his toes, keeping it warm with a fold of skin, and waits. In late winter the chick hatches. The male feeds it a milky substance that he makes in his throat. The female returns to give the chick its first meal of mushed fish, squid and krill. She regurgitates (vomits up) the meal directly into the chick's mouth. For 50 days, the parents take turns staying with the chick while the other goes to sea to feed. Then both parents leave the chick while they go to catch food and bring it back. In early December, the chick starts to **moult**. It leaves the colony to walk to the sea and catch food for itself.

Magnificent Boys

When a female penguin comes back from the sea, she trumpets for her partner. In the mass of penguins, one male recognises that call and scrambles through the crowd. Standing before her, he looks dirty and small, having eaten nothing but a little bit of snow for almost four months. He is proud. He exposes to his partner the small chick that has just hatched and is resting on his feet. She coos and coaxes, and the chick is transferred to her feet. Her entire focus is on the chick. Ignored, exhausted, the male stretches, and then walks out of the colony and 100 kilometres to the ice edge. There he jumps in the water and catches some food.

A magnificent male with a small chick on his feet, awaiting the return of his partner.

The Mottled Coat Crew

The seals of the Antarctic coast and sea-ice regions are a mottled bunch. They feed and sleep in the water, lifting their noses out to breathe every now and then. Often they come out of the sea to rest on floating sea-ice. Young sea-ice seals, called pups, are born on the ice, one pup per mother. Mothers feed their pup incredibly rich milk. Pups get to four times their birth weight in three to four weeks. After this short time, they can go into the water and follow their mums around before starting to fend for themselves.

Rare Ross

The rarest of the sea-ice seals is the **Ross Seal**. They are also the smallest at just 2 metres long and weighing less than 300 kilograms. The biggest are the female Leopard and Weddell Seals, which can weigh 800 kilograms. Ross Seals have a habit of singing while lying on the ice. They expand their throat and produce high-pitched yodels, chirps and chuckles. Ross seals eat fish, squid and krill.

Leaping Leopards

If you saw a **Leopard Seal** slithering over the sea-ice, you might think you were back in the time of dinosaurs. Leopard Seals have many big teeth like a dinosaur and move like reptiles. They have a big head and a patchwork of black-grey-white fur— spotty in places like a land leopard. They eat fish, penguins and other seals. Strangely, though, tiny krill can be their main food.

Female Leopard Seal

Sheets of Light in the Night Sky

In the night sky over Antarctica, you might see shimmering sheets of coloured lights—greens, whites and pinks. The lights are called the Southern Aurora. There is a Northern Aurora as well. Auroras are caused by solar winds made up of high energy particles sent out by the sun. The particles hit the Earth's magnetic field and stream toward the Magnetic Poles. Along the way, they bump into other particles in the air, causing them to light up. The amount of solar wind varies each day. When the sun has many solar flares, the solar wind is strong and you get very pretty auroras.

A Crabeater that Doesn't Eat Crabs

Most **Crabeater Seals** probably never see a crab. They eat krill. When early sealers looked in Crabeater stomachs, they mistook the krill for crab meat and the name stuck. The Crabeater is the most abundant seal in Antarctica. There are 8–20 million of them. Crabeater coats are a creamy colour. They have a dog-like nose. In fact their head almost looks like a Labrador but without the big floppy ears. Male Crabeaters fight a lot and get many scars as they try to attract the attention of a female. The female isn't interested in them until her pup has **weaned**.

Crabeater pup

Weddell I Live

From a distance you could confuse the **Weddell Seal** with a Leopard Seal, but the Weddell Seal has a much smaller head. Its fur is mottled in beautiful, individual patterns. Weddell Seals stay south in winter and live under the ice. They bite through the ice to keep holes open to breathe through. Weddells can hold their breath for 20 minutes or more and chase fish at depths over 600 metres. How long can you hold your breath for? If it takes you 5 seconds to catch each fish, how many fish can you catch on each dive?

Female Weddell Seal and her pup.

Antarctica is
Whale Central

When you think of whales you have to think big. There are two sorts of whales: those with teeth and those without. Whales with teeth hunt big prey, like squid, fish and seals. Whales without teeth eat krill and small fish. Instead of teeth, these whales have a series of brushes, called **baleen**, hanging from the roof of their mouths. When they see a big school of krill, they gulp in a mouthful of seawater and then squish it out through the baleen. The baleen strains out all the krill for the whale to swallow. Some baleen whales eat tonnes of food each day.

Big Baleen Whales

Baleen whales are among the biggest animals ever to have lived on Earth. Here are some baleen whales that live in Antarctica. They range in size from 10 to 30 metres long.

Southern Right Whale

Fin Whale

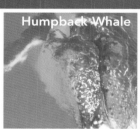
Humpback Whale

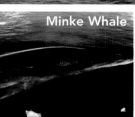
Minke Whale

Sei Whale

Whale or Dolphin?

Killer Whales (Orcas) are actually the largest dolphins, growing to 9 metres long. They live in oceans around the world. In Antarctica they are the top predators, feeding on seals, penguins and other whales, as well as squid and fish. Adult males have a 2-metre high dorsal fin—that's probably taller than your dad. Killer Whales are very intelligent and can learn new hunting techniques. They often hunt in packs, like wolves do, so are called the wolves of the sea.

Whale of a Harvest

Whaling was once a huge industry in Antarctica. Whale **blubber** was used to make oil. Whalers first started hunting Humpback and Southern Right Whales that migrated north. Then they went to hunt the whales that stayed in Antarctica all the time—firstly the biggest, Blue Whales. When Blues became rarer, the whalers targeted the next biggest, the Fin Whales, then the Sei Whales and finally the smaller Minke Whales. Now, Japan is the only country to hunt whales in Antarctica; they catch about 700 each year. Some people see whales as a resource to be harvested; others love whales as intelligent beings that we don't need to kill. What do you think?

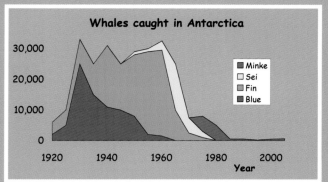

Whales caught in Antarctica

Legend: Minke, Sei, Fin, Blue

The Great Migrate

Many whales **migrate** over big distances. In summer, whales migrate to Antarctica to feed on krill. In winter, they migrate north, often to have their young, called calves, in warmer waters. You can see Humpback and Southern Right Whales from Antarctica around the coast of Australia, New Zealand, South America and Africa.

Southern Right Whale

Whale Tails

You don't get to see much of a whale as it travels along. Just the puff of air and water that it blows out before it takes in a breath and, between the waves, a black area of the whale's back; sometimes you see a fin too. Occasionally, a whale might leap into the air—this is called **breaching**. They make a big splash when they come down. Mostly though, a really good whale sighting will be of the tail. When a whale is finished being near the surface, it arches its back to get a good angle to dive deep, and often lifts its tail out of the water before sliding down below the waves. Scientists can recognise individual whales by the pattern on their tails.

Antarctic Fur Seal
female

Fur Seal family

In late spring, male **Antarctic Fur Seals** come ashore and find territories. Females gather in these and each has a single black pup. Over the next three months, the female goes to sea to feed for a few days then comes back for a few days to give milk to her pup. She keeps doing this for three months, and then the pup is **weaned**.

Antarctic Fur Seal
male

Antarctic Fur Seal pups

A male **Antarctic Fur Seal** with his **harem** and a pup.

Antarctic Fur Coats

Antarctic Fur Seals were hunted almost to extinction by sealers. It took a while, but now their numbers have come back. South Georgia, near the Antarctic Peninsula, is home to about 3 million Antarctic Fur Seals. They feed on whatever is most available to them. Around the island of South Georgia, it is krill.

Homes on Sub-Antarctic Islands

The jewels in the crown of Antarctica are the dozen or so sub-Antarctic islands. These islands are dotted around the Southern Ocean, near the Antarctic Polar Front, and between 500 and 100 kilometres from the continent. A huge number of birds and animals call these islands home.

Three-week-old Elephant Seal pup

Mighty Big Seal

Adult male **Elephant Seals** are the biggest seals in the world—they weigh a whopping 3500 kilograms. Adult females weigh up to 300 kilograms. Females have their first pup when they are about four years old. Newborn pups weigh 45 kilograms—is that more than you weigh now? After three weeks of drinking the rich, fatty milk from their mothers, they weigh about 120 kilograms. From then on, they look after themselves.

Mr Big Nose

The male **Elephant Seal** has a big nose—a bit like a short trunk. At the start of the breeding season, males come ashore and fight each other for a strip of beach. They puff up their nose to scare other males away. If he's lucky, a big male can attract more than 100 females into his **harem**. Males can be big enough to chase other males away from their harems when they are about 12 years old.

When a big male Elephant Seal rears up, he stands over 2.5 metres tall—much taller than your dad.

The Champion Diver

Elephant Seals are great divers. They can stay beneath the water for as long as 90 minutes, although 30 minute dives are more usual. They can easily dive to 800 metres, with the deepest recorded dives being to more than 1.5 kilometres. Elephant Seals feed on squid and lanternfish.

Female Elephant Seal

Sub-Antarctic Penguins

King Penguin chicks

King Penguins

King Penguins are the second biggest penguins, after Emperors. Adults weigh up to 20 kilograms. Like Emperors, each female lays one egg and gives it to the male to **incubate** on his feet. Unlike Emperors, she will return in a few weeks to have her turn at incubating. King Penguin chicks have a shaggy brown coat of down. They look like Russian hats. Kings feed mainly on lanternfish, which they hunt near the **Antarctic Polar Front**.

Rockhopper chicks

Nest Where You Can

Rockhoppers will use whatever is around to build their nests—mud, grass or stones. Some colonies are on flat surfaces, while others are in caves, in thick grass or on unbelievably steep cliffs.

Jumping Punk Penguins

Rockhoppers are feisty little punk penguins. They have red eyes and bright yellow tassels on their heads. Rockies are great jumpers. From a standing start, in a single bound, they can jump their own height. Rockies have a ferocious temperament and fiercely defend their nests against anything that comes along, even if that thing is 50 times their size. Rockhopper chicks, though, are soft, shy little things.

Packing Them In

For **Macaroni Penguins**, when it's time to breed, IT'S TIME TO BREED. One week the colony site may be empty—your voice would echo in it as though you were in the middle of an empty football stadium.

A week later there may be a few hundred birds gathering stones, looking lost in the barren ground.

But after another week it's a crowd (see background picture). Hoards of penguins pour in, trying to get some space and gather stones; the colony is busting at the seams. There are loud discussions over whose stones are whose and who should move their nest a bit further away.

The Most Abundant Penguin

Macaroni Penguins are the most abundant penguins in the world. There are 46 million adult Macaronis. They live in small colonies, or in super-colonies of over a million birds. Each pair defends a small pile of nest stones, just pecking distance away from its neighbours. Can you imagine if one comes home and forgets where her nest is? It would be impossible to find it.

Heard about Heard?

Have you heard of Heard Island, in the Southern Ocean? It's possibly Australia's most isolated bit of land, located south of India and just south of the **Antarctic Polar Front**. Heard Island is 20 kilometres across and 2745 metres high. Its peak, called Mawson Peak, is an active volcano. Its sides are covered by g l a c i e r s; only some coastal areas are ice-free. From a distance, Heard looks like a giant dollop of ice-cream sitting on the ocean.

Plants in the Cold

Sub-Antarctic islands are lush compared to Antarctica. In Antarctica there are only two sorts of flowering plants, about 100 mosses, 350 algae and 400 lichens. But some sub-Antarctic islands have more than 30 flowering plant species. That's lots more than Antarctica, but it's not many really. Your own backyard is likely to have more variety.

Lovely Lichens

Lichens are a hardy bunch. They live in many places. You might have seen some on rocks beside the sea or in the bush. Some lichens in Antarctica actually live inside rocks. Lichens can spread over a surface or stand up like fuzzy grass. They grow slowly and can live for more than 500 years. The more you learn about lichen, the more you end up 'liken' lichen.

Mosses

Mosses like moist, shaded places. If you are in a forest in the Southern Hemisphere, moss can tell you which direction is south. South is on the shady side of trees, and there is more moss on the shady side. In Antarctica, moss can live under snow, where it might be cold but it's also shaded and water can gather there in summer. Moss grows slowly and doesn't like to be disturbed. A footprint on a bed of moss could stay there for years.

Fly or Walk?

Ever heard of a fly that walks? On some **sub-Antarctic** islands lives the Wingless Fly, otherwise known as the 'Walk'. What use are wings on windy little islands? You could get blown out to sea and die. So walks have **evolved** to a life without wings. Mostly, they live on the cabbage-like Pringlia. If walks are disturbed by wind or an animal, they drop to the ground and burrow in—anything to not get blown away.

Algae and Snow Algae

In the ocean around Antarctica and **sub-Antarctic** islands there are many marine algae. Some are **microscopic**, like **phytoplankton**, others can be more than 10 metres long, like kelp. There are also land algae that live in puddles and on wet ground. They can look like moss, but they grow faster so are not as vulnerable to disturbance.

Some algae grow in snow. Banks of snow can turn pink or green with all the algae growing in them.

You may have seen something similar to this kelp on a beach near you. Kelp is also an algae.

Flowering Plants

There aren't many flowering plants in the Antarctic because there are few insects to help pollinate them. The two flowering plants of Antarctica are Antarctic Hair Grass and the cushion plant Antarctic Pearlwort. There are more flowering plants in the sub-Antarctic.

In the sub-Antarctic, **poa** grasses can form large **tussocks,** sometimes metres high. Poa can cover whole islands. Seals like to rest among the tussocks.

*This spiky sub-Antarctic flowering plant is **Acaena**. Its seeds are like arrows and can spear into passing seal fur, penguin feathers or human socks. This gives the seeds a free ride to a new place to grow.*

Pringlia *is a cabbage-like plant once eaten by sealers. It saved many sealers from* **scurvy**, *an illness you can get if you don't eat fresh food. Pringlia tastes a bit like leathery brussel sprouts. Not my favourite green vegetable, how about you? Most sub-Antarctic islands don't have woody plants, like trees and shrubs. It must be too cold for them.*

Fungi

Antarctica is a bit cold for fungi but **sub-Antarctic** islands have lots. We think of mushrooms when we think of fungi, and there are a few of these. But if you leave your sandwiches in your lunch-box for a few weeks, you will see a whole lot of other fungi. Fungi can be bulb-like, hairy, slimy or spongy.

Exploration and Ownership

Early explorers in the Southern Ocean saw enormous **icebergs**. They knew the icebergs must have come from land. So there had to be a large area of land south of them. But the explorers were sailing through stormy seas far from home and in small wooden sailing boats. Can you imagine what a big iceberg could do to one of them? It would crush it. The explorers were not happy to travel too far south.

Cook's Tour

In 1773 Captain James Cook (United Kingdom), following the edge of the **sea-ice**, sailed all the way around Antarctica without seeing land. But he was the first to cross the **Antarctic Circle**. The first people to see Antarctica were the crew of a Russian boat skippered by Captain Fabian von Bellingshausen, in 1820. Just one year later, Captain John Davis and his crew from the United States stepped ashore.

Captain James Cook

The Antarctic Pie

Some nations decided to raise their flags and claim chunks of Antarctica. Slices of Antarctica were claimed by the United Kingdom (1908), New Zealand (1923), France (1924), Australia (1933), Norway (1939), Chile (1940) and Argentina (1943). Confusingly, three nations claimed the Antarctic Peninsula (Chile, Argentina and the United Kingdom). Things calmed down with the signing of the Antarctic Treaty in 1959. Under the treaty, nations with claims won't enforce them and no new claims will be made. More than 40 nations have now signed the treaty and it has led to an era of co-operation on the frozen continent.

A proud Argentinian expeditioner waves his country's flag at an Argentine station in Antarctica.

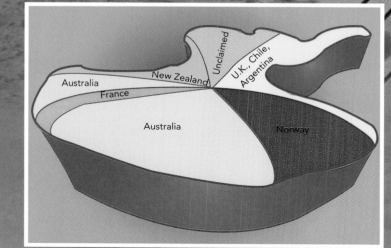

Doing It the Hard Way

Early explorers travelled in small wooden boats through dangerous icy seas to Antarctica. They took plain, not very tasty food and maybe one change of clothes. Once on shore, they often marched for weeks through snow and over hard ice, dragging heavy sleds. During winter, months without sun made them feel like they were going crazy. And their families were far away. These blokes were doing it the hard way.

Australian stamps commemorating the early explorer Douglas Mawson.

Shackleton's hut (1907) on Ross Island

Inside Shackleton's hut

Me First! Me First!

One goal of early explorers was to be first to the **Geographic South Pole**: Robert Scott (United Kingdom, 1901 and 1910), Ernest Shackleton (United Kingdom, 1907) and Roald Amundson (Norway, 1910) all tried. Roald Amundsen got there first on 14 December 1911. In 1909 three Australians, Tannant David, Alistair Mackay and Douglas Mawson, became the first people to reach the **Magnetic South Pole**. Ernest Shackleton decided he hadn't done enough hard things so in 1914 he planned to cross the continent by foot. Unfortunately, his ship got crushed in the **sea-ice** of the Weddell Sea. Amazingly, after an epic adventure over the ice and across the ocean in small boats, all members of the expedition survived.

A Foot in the Door

In 1898 a bunch of guys decided they would like to spend a year ashore. Would you like to have been one of them? The group, comprising mostly Norwegians, was led by Carstons Borchgrevink to Cape Adare, near the Ross Sea. One team member, a zoologist called Nicolai Hanson, became famous as the first person to die on Antarctica. The group, including Louis Bernacchi, the first Australian to winter in Antarctica, lived through the winter months in a little hut (right) that is still standing, after over 100 years.

New buildings at today's modern Orcadas Station

In 1902 William Bruce from Scotland packed his kilt and headed to the cold south to set up the first long-term station. He chose an island in the South Orkneys, near the Antarctic Peninsula. At the end of the expedition, Bruce offered his station to the United Kingdom, but they didn't want it. Argentina did though. They named the station Orcadas and have lived there ever since.

Expeditioners watch as their ship tries to penetrate the Antarctic ice and reach the continent.

Station Life

Over the past 100 years, many stations have been built in Antarctica. The longest permanently occupied station on the continent is Mawson (Australia), which was established in 1954.

How Would You Like to Live in Antarctica?

Antarctic stations are quite comfortable. You have your own room, a big community movie room and a spacious kitchen where a chef cooks delicious meals for you. Buildings at the station include the living quarters, workshops and science laboratories. Networks of above-ground pipes connect the buildings, bringing water for heating and electricity from the station generator.

*A **blizzard** blasts in over Mawson Station in Antarctica.*

Getting Around

There are lots of ways to get around in Antarctica. You can ski or ride a four-wheel motorbike. Over greater distances, you can drive a **Hägglunds**. A Hägglunds is even able to stay afloat if it breaks through the sea-ice into the water. For long-distance travel inland, you could drive a bulldozer, or take to the sky in a helicopter.

A Hägglunds afloat after accidentally breaking through thin sea-ice.

Keeping in Touch

Living in Antarctica you are isolated from direct contact with family, friends, pets and the hobbies you love. You can't go to the beach for a swim, for example. But you can make new friends and have unique experiences. Communication is good these days, with satellite connections 24 hours a day. There is a telephone beside your bed and you can call anywhere anytime. You have email access and can log on to the internet. Before satellite communication, there was radio contact, and before that, you just had to wait for the next ship to come in with a mail bag.

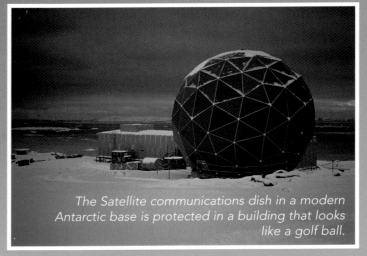

The Satellite communications dish in a modern Antarctic base is protected in a building that looks like a golf ball.

Radios in the communications room of an old Antarctic base.

Who Lives There?

Most expeditioners to Antarctica are involved with station maintenance and science support. It's a harsh environment, so carpenters, plumbers, electricians and diesel mechanics are kept busy making sure everything works. There are also scientists who do research in biology (the study of living creatures), meteorology (the study of climate), atmospheric physics (the study of what happens in the air above the clouds) and geology (the study of rocks). Expeditioners wear layers of clothing especially designed to keep them warm and mobile for the tasks they need to do.

Dogs were once important for long-distance travel in Antarctica but the last dogs left in the early 1990s.

How We View
Antarctica

The first people who went to Antarctica saw it as a place that they could take whatever they wanted from. We think differently about Antarctica now. How might people view Antarctica in 50 years time? We don't know. But they might be disappointed if we don't look after it now.

A Holiday in Antarctica?

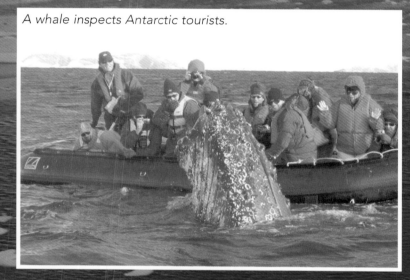
A whale inspects Antarctic tourists.

The scenery and wildlife of Antarctica are spectacular and unique. Each year more people are going there to have a look. Some years, there are more than 20 000 people heading south across the Southern Ocean. There are another 10 000 or more people going down as expeditioners. Hopefully, these people love the places they see, take only photographs and memories, and leave only footsteps in the snow.

A passenger ship cruises through ice-filled seas near the Antarctic Peninsula.

Saving Antarctica

People from around the world are now working together to try and protect Antarctica. To protect wildlife, for example, there is an international Commission for the Conservation of Antarctic Marine Living Resources (CCAMLR). Mining and mineral exploration is prohibited in Antarctica until at least the year 2041. The release of chemicals that might have caused a hole in the protective ozone layer over Antarctica is banned. What happens in Antarctica affects the whole planet. That includes global warming. Although change in the Antarctic is slow, if the temperature got much warmer, a lot more ice would melt, causing the sea level to rise quickly.

Exploitation

Antarctica was first seen as a place to be **exploited**. Sealers came and took the seals. They were followed by explorers wishing to claim land. Then whalers killed so many whales that some species almost became extinct. Harvesting of whales in Antarctic waters was the biggest fishery the world has ever seen. After whaling finished, fisheries started catching various fish species, squid and Antarctic krill. We actually don't know what the Southern Ocean was like before humans went there, because we changed it so much before starting to research and understand it.

*An abandoned whale-processing factory on **sub-Antarctic** South Georgia Island.*

Activities

1. Name some lands that once were part of Gondwana. (pages 8–9)

2. Why is Antarctica called the highest continent? (pages 10–11)

3. How could you use ice-cores from Antarctica to measure changes in the Earth's air? (pages 12–13)

4. Explain how Antarctic **sea-ice** forms, thickens and breaks up each year? (pages 14–15)

5. Describe three sorts of **zooplankton** that live in the ocean around Antarctica. (pages 16–17)

6. How do some Antarctic fish stop their blood from freezing? (pages 18–19)

7. What do Burrowing Petrels do to try to avoid hungry Skuas? (pages 20–21)

8. Why are seabirds vulnerable to long-line fishing? (pages 22–23)

9. Where does a clever male Adelie Penguin build his nest? (pages 24–25)

10. Why do Emperor Penguins huddle? (pages 26–27)

11. How can you tell a Weddell Seal from a Leopard Seal? What do both eat? (pages 28–29)

12. What are the two groups of whales and how do they catch food? (pages 30–31)

13. Name a whale that feeds in Antarctica during winter than migrates north and out of Antarctic waters in summer. Have you seen one of these? (pages 30–31)

14. What's the difference in the pup-raising methods of Elephant Seals and Antarctic Fur Seals. (pages 32–33)

15. What penguin is most abundant and where does it live, Antarctica or the **sub-Antarctic?** (pages 32–33)

16. What sort of an animal is a 'walk' and why is it called a walk? (pages 36–37)

17. If a snow patch turned a pink colour, what could be the reason? (pages 36–37)

18. Who were the first people to stand at the Magnetic South Pole? What would you have to be on to stand at the Magnetic South Pole today? (pages 38–39)

19. If you were an expeditioner to Antarctica, what job would you like to have and why? (pages 40–41)

20. What animals are hunted by fishermen in Antarctica today? (pages 42–43)

Glossary (what words mean)

Amphipod Group of small **crustaceans** living in water—includes sea-lice. They have a hard **exoskeleton** around their bodies.

Antarctic Circle Line of latitude at 66°33'S, south of which there are summer days when the sun never sets and winter days when the sun never rises.

Antarctic ice-sheet Thick layer of ice over Antarctica, formed by the accumulation of thousands of years of snowfall.

Antarctic Polar Front Region of the Southern Ocean where cold Antarctic surface water drops below warmer northern waters.

Baleen Horny plates that hang from the upper jaw of some whales and form a filter through which water passes but food does not.

Blubber Fat that forms a layer under the skin; very thick in whales.

Blizzard Strong wind filled with so much blowing snow that it is difficult to see anything more than a metre in front of you.

Breaching When whales dive out of the water.

Conductivity Ability to carry an electric current. The more salt there is in water, the better it conducts electricity.

Continental shelf The submerged edge of a continent.

Copepod The most common group of small crustaceans living in water. They have long antennae on their heads with which they 'breast-stroke'.

Crust The crust of the Earth is its outermost layer. There are two sorts of crust: continental crust, which is relatively light but sometimes quite thick—this is the land; and oceanic crust, which is thin but heavy.

Crustacean Animals with hard **exoskeleton**s—includes crabs and prawns.

Denser More dense, thicker and heavier.

Evolve Gradually change over time to better suit conditions you live in.

Exoskeleton A skeleton worn on the outside, like a body shell.

Exploitation Using something to benefit you but not the thing you are exploiting.

Fledge When chicks leave their parents and look after themselves.

Fluorescent Glows in the dark.

Geographic South Pole Southernmost point of the Earth, around which the Earth rotates.

Glacier A river of ice.

Glacier tongue The end of a glacier that is floating in the ocean.

Hägglunds (pronounced Hag-lands) A Swedish-built, two-cabin vehicle that drives on tracks (like a bulldozer), has comfortable seats and is powered by an eight-cylinder, diesel engine. Great for travel on snow and ice.

Harem A group of females belonging to one male.

Iceberg A large piece of ice in the ocean that has broken off a glacier or ice-shelf.

Ice-shelf A large floating section of ice formed from an ice-sheet or many glacier tongues joined together.

Incubate When a bird sits on an egg to keep it warm until the chick hatches out.

Lava Hot, liquid rock from below the Earth's crust. Lava is the red stuff that comes out of volcanoes.

Magnetic South Pole Where lines in the Earth's magnetic field are vertical. The south end of a compass points to this location. This pole moves. One hundred years ago, it was on Antarctica but today it is about 100 kilometres offshore and towards New Zealand.

Microscopic Tiny things you can only see through a microscope.

Migrate When animals travel from one place to another, often seasonally.

Moult Shedding feathers, hair or exoskeleton as a new body covering grows.

Nutrient Something that provides nourishment. Nutrient-rich waters contain lots of particles that are important for phytoplankton to grow.

Parasites Animals or plants that live on or in other living things.

Photosynthesis The process by which plants use energy in sunlight to make food.

Phytoplankton Microscopic plants that drift in water.

Scavenger An animal that feeds on animals that are dead.

Sea-ice Ice that forms on the sea surface if the temperature of the sea drops below –1.8°C.

Slurry A mixture of liquids and suspended solids. Smashed-up ice in water is one sort of slurry.

Solar wind Massive amounts of energised particles that are continually being sent out from the sun.

Solar flare A major eruption of flames and heat on the surface of the sun.

Sub-Antarctic A region of the Southern Ocean in the vicinity of the Antarctic Polar Front.

Subduction zone Where a section of the Earth's crust is forced down underneath another section.

Wean When baby mammals stop getting milk from their mothers.

Zooplankton Tiny animals that drift in the ocean and eat phytoplankton or each other.

Want to Know More?

Websites

classroomantarctica.aad.gov.au

www.aad.gov.au

www.antarctica.ac.uk

www.antarctica.org.nz

www.antarcticanz.govt.nz

www.antarcticaonline.com/antarctica/home/home.htm

www.coolantarctica.com

www.earthinstitute.columbia.edu

www.enchantedlearning.com/school/Antarctica

www.discoveringantarctica.org.uk

www.lonelyplanet.com/worldguide/destinations/antarctica

http://www.66degreessouth.org

Books

Bowden, T. (1997) *The Silence Calling: Australians in Antarctica 1947-97*. Allen & Unwin, Sydney, Australia.

Carey, P. and Franklin, C. (2006) *Antarctica Cruising Guide*. Awa Press, Wellington, New Zealand.

Poncet, S. and Crosbie, K. (2005) *A Visitors Guide to South Georgia*. WildGuides, Maidenhead, England.

Hooper, M. (2000) *Antarctic Journal: The Hidden Worlds of Antarctica's animals*. Francis Lincoln, London, England.

Shirihai, H. (2002) *A Complete Guide to Antarctic Wildlife: the Birds and Marine Mammals of the Antarctic Continent and Southern Ocean*. Alula Press, Finland.

Rubin, J. (1996) *Antarctica*. Lonely Planet Publications, Melbourne, Australia.

Trewby, M. (2002) *Antarctica: an Encyclopedia from Abbott Ice Shelf to Zooplankton*. Firefly Books, Auckland, New Zealand.

Tulloch, C. (2007) *Antarctica: The Heart of the World*. ABC Books, Sydney, Australia.

What's in a Name?

All animals have at least one 'common name' and a scientific or Latin name. For example the Antarctic Fur Seal's scientific name is Arctocephalus gazella. Because common names for one animal can vary, if you want to know more about an animal, it's best to look it up under its scientific name. All the animals pictured in this book are listed in the index with both their common names and their scientific names.

Index